THE CLIFF

BARBADOS

RECIPES BY PAUL OWENS

published by

Miller Publishing Company
Edghill, St Thomas
Barbados, West Indies
Tel: (246) 421 6700
e-mail: miller@caribsurf.com

Miller Publishing Company

Photographed entirely by Artie
Tel: (246) 422 3776
e-mail: artie@artiephotography.com
www.artiephotography.com

Graphic Design and Layout by
Alison Forde Alleyne
LoBa Design & Advertising INC
Tel: (246) 230 4153 or (246) 423 7196
e-mail: zebe@sunbeach.net

LoBa Design & Advertising INC

ISBN 976 - 8078 - 97 - 9

Special thanks to Brian Ward, Peter Harris, the management and the staff of THE CLIFF

the people who make it happen at
THE CLIFF

The Cliff

First opened in 1995, The Cliff has established itself as
one of the very finest and most popular restaurants in the entire Caribbean.
To list the names of all the international celebrities who have been
to The Cliff would not only perhaps seem a little tacky, it would also be
impossible because of the limited space available on this page.
Suffice it to say that a veritable 'Who's Who' of members of royal families;
world statesmen; stars of screen, stage and the sports arena;
and some of the world's most successful business personalities have
all dined here over the years, with many of them returning on more
than one occasion.

The Cliff, located right on the edge of the sea,
has a wonderful location and it has been cleverly designed to make the
most of the magical ambience created by its surroundings.
Yet, when first time diners recall their experiences at The Cliff, the first
thing that usually comes to mind is the food that they were served.

Chef Paul Owens consistently creates an eclectic variety of
exquisite dishes; a truly tempting range that always makes choosing
from his menu a challenging task. Paul has a special flair for
combining contrasting flavours and textures, which together add up to
deliciously interesting cuisine.
He is also a master of the art of presentation.

Not the kind of person to allow success to go to his head,
Paul's philosophy is that his reputation is only as good as the next dish
to leave his kitchen. Bearing this in mind, he works very hard to maintain
his standards at all times, paying great attention to even the smallest detail.

Born in Liverpool, England, Paul Owens has lived in Barbados for some 15
years. Throughout that time he has been followed by a dedicated
band of lovers of good food as he moved from one restaurant to another,
and then to The Cliff, where he has really made his name.
Written up in many of the leading catering magazines, and virtually
all of the top newstand publications, Paul has been given rave reviews
on each of the many occassions that he has been featured.
He has also appeared on a number of television programmes.

Despite his enormous success, Paul remains a modest and
very down to earth person. He is happy to share some of his collection
of outstanding recipes with you in this book.

18 July 2002
To Hilary Peterson
Best Wishes

Chef

If you can't stand the heat

stay out of the kitchen

appetizers

tartare of scallops
coriander cream
* coriander vinaigrette * coriander oil

Finely dice the scallops and put in a small bowl,

season with a little salt and pepper.

Add a teaspoon of olive oil, a little chilli and some capers.

Fit tightly into a 3" x 1" mould in the

centre of the plate and allow to set.

Remove the mould and attractively

surround the scallops with the coriander cream,

vinaigrette and oil.

Cut the wonton skins into fine strips

and deep fry for about one minute.

Sprinkle them around the edge of the plate

along with some coriander leaves, capers and

diced tomato.

Serve with hot toast.

8-10 oz fresh scallops
pinch chilli flakes
salt & freshly ground black pepper
coriander leaves
capers
1 diced tomato
wonton skins (optional)
virgin olive oil
coriander cream (p106 *1)
coriander vinaigrette (p106 *2)
coriander oil (p106 *3)

Chef's Note . . .

The best way to decorate a plate with creams and

sauces is to use a squeezy plastic dispenser, such as

those used for ketchup. This gives better control.

snow crab cake
with chargrilled red & yellow pepper vinaigrette * red curry oil

Heat a little butter in a non-stick frying pan. Squeeze any moisture from the crabmeat. Add chopped shallots to the butter and saute for 1 minute. Add the crab and cook for 2 minutes constantly stirring. Remove crab and allow to cool. When cool, mix the crab with the potato, tarragon and parsley. Season to taste and form into 4 to 6 cakes. Coat the cakes in the flour, then egg wash, then breadcrumbs.

1¹/₂ cups snow crab meat

1 cup prepared mash potatoes

1 tbsp chopped tarragon

3 shallots, diced

salt & freshly ground black pepper

1 tbsp chopped parsley

16 coriander leaves

oil for frying

breadcrumbs

flour

egg wash (1 egg in 1 cup of milk)

red & yellow pepper vinaigrettte

(p109 *19)

Curry Oil

2 tbsp red curry paste

1 cup olive oil

4 tbsp sherry wine vinegar

For the Curry Oil

Place the paste, olive oil and vinegar into a blender and puree until smooth. Salt and pepper to taste. Place into a squeezy bottle.

For the Salsa refer to index (p108 *17)

To Assemble

Heat the vegetable oil at 350. Deep fry the crab cake until golden brown. Squeeze the Red and Yellow pepper vinaigrette attractively on four plates. Spoon a little curry oil around. Place the crab cake in the centre of the plate and top with the salsa. Surround with the coriander leaves.

grilled portobello mushroom
salad with asparagus,
* white truffle vinaigrette

Saute the mushrooms in hot butter for about 2 minutes each side.
Allow to cool.

Blanch the asparagus in boiling salted water for
about 1-2 minutes; shock in ice water and chill.

Mix the vinaigrette (see index).

Chargrill the mushrooms and asparagus,
cut tomatoes into quarters and de-seed.

Rub the tomatoes with olive oil and grill for
1 minute each side.

Allow to cool.

Put a little olive oil on the lettuce and
arrange in the centre of four plates. Slice the
warm mushrooms into 4 pieces and arrange
around lettuce.

Top with the asparagus and tomatoes.

Using a squeezy bottle, drizzle the vinaigrette
over the salad and sprinkle with grated parmesan
cheese and chopped shallots.

Top with parmesan shavings.

**4 medium sized
portobello mushrooms
12 asparagus spears
4 cups mesclun lettuce
4 plum tomatoes
2 oz parmesan shavings
4-6 fl.oz white truffle vinaigrette
(p109 *18)
4 oz butter
4 oz grated parmesan cheese
chopped shallots**

smoked salmon, cream cheese & spinach ravioli
* garlic cream sauce

Mix the cream cheese, herbs and garlic and season with salt and pepper. Using a tablespoon, spoon 4 separate heaps in the centre of 4 squares of pasta. Top the cream cheese with smoked salmon and blanched spinach.

Brush the pasta with the egg yolk and place the remaining sheet on top. Squeeze with fingers firmly until sealed.

Using a 4" round pastry cutter, cut out the ravioli and blanch in boiling, salted water for 75 seconds. Plunge into ice water. Wrap in cling film and refrigerate until required.

Reduce the garlic cream sauce to a syrupy consistency. Place the ravioli in boiling salted water for a further $1^{1}/_{2}$ minutes. Remove with a slotted spoon. Dry on a kitchen towel. Place in the centre of the bowls. Pour over the sauce and sprinkle with parmesan cheese. Garnish with diced smoked salmon, a leaf of basil and blanched spinach.

8 5" x 5" sheets fresh pasta
4 x 2 oz slices smoked salmon
4 x slithers smoked salmon for garnish
4 tbsp cream cheese
2 cloves garlic (chopped)
12 spinach leaves
(blanched and chilled)
1 tbsp chopped parsley
2 tsp dried italian seasoning
2 cups garlic cream sauce (see p38)
$^{1}/_{2}$ cup grated parmesan
4 tbsp tomato concasse
4 sprigs of basil
2 egg yolks
a little flour for coating

spicy cherry
tomato gazpacho

Combine the tomatoes, bell peppers, coriander,
jalepeno, tomato juice and half the cucumbers in a bowl.
In a food processor, puree the remaining cucumber,
lime juice and bread. Add this to the tomato mixture
and season to taste. Place in the refrigerator
and serve chilled. Garnish with sliced avocado, fresh
coriander, cherry tomatoes and garlic croutons.

4 cups cherry tomatoes,
peeled, seeded and diced
1 red sweet pepper,
seeded and diced
1 yellow sweet pepper,
seeded and diced
3 cups of tomato juice
1 jalepeno pepper, minced
2 cucumbers, peeled and diced
4 slices of bread
juice of 2 limes
$1/2$ cup of coriander, chopped
salt & freshly ground black pepper

To garnish - sliced avocado, fresh coriander,
cherry tomatoes, garlic croutons

smoked salmon &
warm new potato salad
* horseradish cream * horseradish oil

Cook potatoes in salted boiling water until soft.

Allow to cool and cut in half, brush with the

olive oil and sprinkle with snipped chives.

Dribble a little olive oil over the lettuce

and arrange in the centre of 4 plates.

Top with the sliced smoked salmon.

Arrange the horseradish cream around the salad,

garnished with quartered cherry tomatoes.

Warm the new potatoes in the microwave

for 30-40 seconds, place attractively around

the plate and top with chopped chives.

Dribble the horseradish oil over the top.

Top with the caviar if using.

8 x 2 oz slices smoked salmon

4 cups meslun greens

12 new potatoes

4 fl.oz horseradish oil (p106 *4)4

fl.oz horseradish cream (p106 *5)

sprinkling snipped chives

4 cherry tomatoes

a little virgin olive oil

4 tbsp caviar (optional)

rocket & goats cheese salad

* balsamic vinaigrette

Wash the rocket leaves and set aside.

Put the goats cheese in a stainless steel bowl over boiling water and stir continuously until smooth. This removes the grains. Stir in the mixed herbs and allow to cool. Mix a little olive oil, balsamic vinegar, diced shallots, chopped garlic and salt and pepper. Add the vegetables and leave in a cool place for 1 hour. Remove the vegetables and chargrill for 1 minute each side.

Allow to cool.

4 cups rocket leaves
olive oil
12 tsp goats cheese
2 tsp mixed herbs
balsamic vinaigrette (p106 *6)
balsamic reduction (p106 *7)
goats cheese cream (p107 *8)
$^1/_2$ cup tomato concasse

Grilled Vegetables
1 medium size zucchini
1 medium size egg plant
1 each of red and yellow peppers
2 medium beetroots
(cooked and peeled)
2 fl.oz olive oil
1 fl.oz balsamic vinegar
2 tbsp diced shallots
1 tbsp chopped garlic
salt & freshly ground black pepper
garlic croutons (see recipe p34)

To assemble, place some grilled vegetables in the centre of 4 plates. Rub the rocket with a little olive oil. Arrange on top of the vegetables. Using squeezy bottles, squeeze some balsamic vinaigrette and goats cheese cream around the plate. Sprinkle tomato concasse on the dressing. Mould the goats cheese into quenelles using two teaspoons or simply sprinkle over the salad. Add some garlic croutons. Finally squeeze some balsamic reduction over the salad and serve.

salmon spring roll
*chive cream sauce

Blanch the spinach leaves in boiling salted water for 30 seconds, put into ice water. Repeat with the carrots until just cooked. Put the vegetables between two pieces of kitchen paper towels to absorb the water. Dry the vegetables. Salt and pepper the salmon. Wrap each piece of salmon with two spinach leaves and two pieces of carrot. Lay a spring roll wrapper in a diamond position on a flat surface. Brush the corners with the egg yolk. Place the salmon at the bottom point of the wrapper, fold the wrapper over the salmon, then fold the two sides into the centre and roll to form neat spring rolls.

4 x 2 oz pieces salmon
8 spinach leaves
8 thin slices of carrots
seasoned mashed potato

Chive Cream Sauce
2 tbsp diced shallots
1 cup white wine
1 cup fish stock
1$^{1}/_{2}$ cups heavy cream
juice of half a lemon
$^{1}/_{4}$ cup snipped chives
4 spring roll wrappers
1 egg yolk
oil for frying

For the Sauce

Reduce the white wine and shallots by half, add fish stock and reduce by half. Add the cream and boil down to a syrupy consistency. Add lemon juice and chives, season to taste.

To serve

Put a little mashed potato in the centre of the plate. Cook the spring roll in hot oil for about 3-4 minutes at 350 degrees. When ready put on kitchen paper to blot the oil. Pour a litte sauce around the potatoes. Cut the salmon roll on an angle and press into the potato and serve.

tuna tartare
* asian vinaigrette * chilli oil
* sesame soy emulsion

Mix tuna with sesame seeds, lemon juice, salt and pepper, chilli powder and olive oil. Taste for seasoning and spiciness and refrigerate.

To assemble the dish

Place a 2"x 1" pastry cutter in the centre of the plate and fill with the tuna tartare mixture. Remove the pastry cutter and surround with the asian vinaigrette, a little chilli oil and the sesame soy emulsion. Sprinkle a little chopped chives, tomato concasse and coriander leaves around the plate and serve.

Additional decorations in photo are fried wonton skins and fried nori seaweed.

12 oz finely diced sushi grade tuna
2 tbsp lemon juice
pinch chilli powder
salt & freshly ground black pepper
1 tsp toasted black sesame seeds
a few leaves of fresh coriander
a little olive oil
asian vinaigrette (p107 *9)
chilli oil (p107 *10)
sesame soy emulsion (p107 *11)

spicy caesar salad
with crispy bacon
& shaved parmesan

Lay the bacon rashers on a baking sheet and cook
in 350 degree oven until golden and very crispy.
Keep at room temp. Mix the romaine leaves with
the olive oil and a little chili flakes, keep chilled.
Put the romaine in the centre of the plates.
Using a squeezy bottle, squeeze the dressing
over and around the lettuce.
Sprinkle with the parmesan, bacon
and crispy crouton. Dribble a little olive oil
around the lettuce and sprinkle with the
tomato concasse.

4 romaine hearts
caesar dressing (p107 *12)
pinch red chilli flakes
parmesan shavings
4 oz grated parmesan
4 tbsp virgin olive oil
$^1/_2$ cup garlic croutons (see p34)
8 strips of back bacon
$^1/_2$ cup tomato concasse

thai seafood salad
with lemon grass * japanese noodles & coriander

Poach the seafood separately in a pot of simmering
salted water for 2 minutes.
Allow to cool and mix together.

12 scallops

4 oz squid (cleaned)

12 shrimp

4 cups mixed lettuce

2 cups cooked udon noodles

(or any kind of noodles)

$^1/_2$ cup chopped coriander

1 cup red and yellow bell peppers

(cut into julienne strips)

10 cherry tomatoes cut in half

1 thinly sliced cucumber

1 cup coriander leaves

For the Dressing

4 fl.oz fish sauce

4 fl.oz lemon juice

2 tbsp of very finely diced lemon grass

1 pinch chilli flakes

Mix the fish sauce, lemon grass,
lemon juice and chilli flakes.

Add the liquid to the seafood and mix in
tomatoes, cucumber, coriander, noodles and
peppers. Arrange lettuce in the centre of
4 plates and top with the seafood mixture.
Top with extra coriander and julienne strips of
red and yellow bell peppers before serving.

Chef's Note . . .
If you find the sauce too tart,
you can add a little sugar.

pumpkin & ginger soup

Place all the ingredients, except the cream, into a pot

and bring to boil. Lower heat and simmer for 20-25 minutes.

When cool, blend the soup.

Reheat the soup and season to taste.

Add the cream just before serving.

Garnish with garlic croutons,

diced carrots and pumpkin.

4 cups pumpkin

1 cup carrots

$1/2$ cup celery

$1/4$ cup ginger

1 cup onions

8 cups chicken stock

1 bunch marjoram

salt & freshly ground black pepper

$1^1/_2$ cups cream

For the Garlic Croutons

Using a serated edged knife, cut the bread

into $1/4$ inch cubes. Mix the olive oil and garlic

together. Place the bread into a bowl and

mix with the olive oil. Place the bread on

a baking sheet and season with freshly

ground salt and pepper. Place in a preheated

oven until golden and crisp.

Garlic Croutons

4 slices white sandwich bread

2 cloves garlic, chopped

4 tbsp olive oil

salt & freshly ground black pepper

carpaccio of dolphin
with honey & soy
warm beansprouts, ginger
& spring onions

12 oz dolphin, thinly sliced

$^1/_2$ cup soy sauce

juice of 2 lemons

4 tbsp honey

4 tbsp toasted sesame seeds

4 tbsp chopped coriander

tomato concasse

8 -10 oz beansprouts

$1^1/_2$ tbsp pickled ginger

3 oz spring onions

2 fl.oz olive oil

salt & freshly ground black pepper

For the sauce whisk together the soy sauce, lemon juice, honey, half the sesame seeds and the chopped coriander.

Lay the sliced dolphin in the centre of the plate. Dribble a little sauce over the dolphin and chill. Heat a little olive oil in a non-stick frying pan until very hot.

Add the beansprouts and season with a little salt and pepper. When the sprouts begin to wilt, add the spring onions and the ginger.

Place the warm beansprouts on top of the chilled dolphin and garnish with coriander leaves and tomato concasse. Serve at once.

Chef's Note . . .

When using raw fish, it is essential to use the best quality fresh fish available.

Please Note . . .
The fish known in Barbados as dolphin IS NOT the mammal, also known as a porpoise, of the 'Flipper' variety.

...th smoked salmon

...arlic cream sauce

...an

Cook the linguine in lots of salted, boiling water
for 8-10 minutes and drain.

For the Sauce
Bring the white wine to a boil
and reduce by half. Add the chicken stock
and reduce a further five minutes.
Add the cream and stir in the garlic butter.
Season with salt and pepper and
reduce to a syrupy consistency.
Add the linguine and toss in
the smoked salmon.
Place the pasta in 4 bowls and
sprinkle with parmesan, parsley,
chives and tomato concasse.

Chef's Note . . .
There is no substitute for fresh parmesan.

1 lb linguine
12 oz smoked salmon
cut into strips
$^1/_2$ cup tomato concasse
$^1/_2$ cup snipped chives
4 oz grated parmesan cheese

Garlic Cream Sauce
1 cup white wine
2 cups chicken stock
2 cups heavy cream
3 oz hard garlic butter
salt & freshly ground black pepper

lobster & salt cod cake
* sweetcorn & basil sauce
* crispy leeks

8 oz lobster tail (cooked)

1 cup salt cod

2 tbsp parsley (chopped)

3 tbsp olive oil

1 cup mashed potato

a little butter for cooking the cakes

a little crushed black pepper

12 spinach leaves

1 leek cut in juliennes

Sweetcorn & Basil Sauce (p107 *13)

Soak the salt cod for 3 hours and
repeat the process about 4 times.
Cover the salt cod once again with cold water
and bring to a boil and repeat this process 3 times.
This is to remove the salt from the fish.
While the fish is warm, shred it in a food
processor until flaky.
Place into a stainless steel bowl
and mix with the mashed potato.
Add the parsley and the black pepper.
Cut the lobster meat into quarter inch cubes
and add to the salt cod mixture.
Mix well and form into 4-6 small cakes.

Sautee the lobster cakes with a little butter
until brown and heated through
- about 4 minutes each side. Pour the sweetcorn
and basil sauce (p107 *13) into 4 bowls and place
the lobster cake in the centre. Top the cake with
fried leeks and a basil leaf. Garnish with blanched
spinach and serve.

chinese roast pork
with moo shu pancakes
* cucumber * spring onions * hoi sin sauce

Marinate the pork in the hoi sin and soy sauce over night.

Roast the pork at 350 degrees for 40 minutes and allow to cool.

Brush one side of each pancake with a little sesame oil and
join the pancakes with the oiled sides together.

Cut the pork into strips. Shred the spring onions.

Heat the pancakes in the microwave for 20 seconds.

Separate the pancakes and spread a little hoi sin
sauce over them. Put the pork in the centre,
top with onion and cucumber and roll up.

Cut each roll in half and serve with a little
hoi sin sauce on the side.

8 moo shu pancakes

1 lb trimmed pork tenderloin

8 tbsp hoi sin sauce

2 tbsp soy sauce

4 tsp sesame oil

4-6 oz spring onions
(cut into julienne strips)

2 english cucumbers
(cut into julienne strips)

Chef's Note . . .
The reason for oiling the pancakes is to
keep them moist, as they dry out quickly.

open ravioli of scallops
with tomato fondue
* pesto cream sauce

12 large scallops

8 5" x 5" sheets pasta

8 tbsp grated parmesan cheese

Pesto Cream Sauce

3 cups garlic cream sauce (see p38)

4-6 tbsp basil pesto (p108 *16)

Tomato Fondue

1/2 lb fresh tomatoes

2 cloves garlic (chopped)

2 tbsp tomato paste

3 oz sugar

1 small onion

4 oz white wine

6 oz basil cut into strips

salt & freshly ground black pepper

4 sprigs of basil

For the Tomato Fondue - Chop tomato and onion and lightly saute in a little olive oil until soft. (Do not color). Add finely chopped garlic and tomato paste. Mix well, then allow to cook for just a few minutes. Add the wine and the sugar. Mix well and place in a pre-heated oven at 350 degrees for 30 minutes, covered with a lid. When cooked remove from oven and whisk in a handful of chopped basil.

For the Sauce - Put the garlic sauce in a saucepan and boil. Reduce to a syrupy consistency and stir in the pesto and season to taste.

For the Pasta - If using fresh pasta, follow the recipe from page 38. If using dried pasta, cook according to instructions and keep warm.

Assembly - Saute the scallops in a hot pan with a little butter for about 2 minutes each side. You want the scallops slightly undercooked. Put a sheet of pasta on the bottom of the bowl and place a tablespoon of fondue in the centre. Pour a little pesto sauce around the bowl and arrange 3 scallops attractively around the fondue and sprinkle with a little grated parmesan cheese. Top with the remaining sheet of pasta. Place another tablespoon of fondue on top of the pasta, sprinkle with parmesan cheese, top with a sprig of basil and serve.

asparagus & mushrooms
in a puff pastry case
* wild mushroom sauce

20 spears of asparagus
2 cups button mushrooms
1 sheet of all butter puff pastry
2 oz melted butter

Wild Mushroom Sauce
1 cup madeira wine
2 cups chicken stock
1¹/₂ cups heavy cream
1 cup dried cepes
salt & freshly ground black pepper
1 egg yolk

Peel the asparagus and blanch in salted boiling water for 1¹/₂ minutes .
Cool in ice water and chill. Place the pastry sheet on a cool surface and
brush with the egg yolk. Using a three inch pastry cutter, cut out
4 circles. Place on a greased baking pan and bake in a hot oven
345-350 degrees for 20 minutes until golden and flaky.
Best to be cooked in advance. Saute the button
mushrooms in the butter with salt and pepper.
Keep warm.

For the Sauce - Bring the wine to a boil then add the
chicken stock. Reduce by half then add the dried
cepes, the cream and salt and pepper. Reduce for
15 minutes and strain. Discard the cepes. Cut the
pastries in half horizontally and reduce the sauce
to a syrupy consistency.

Warm the asparagus in boiling water for
30 seconds. Put a little sauce in the centre of 4
plates. Place the bottom half of the pastry case on
the sauce, spoon some of the sauteed button
mushrooms onto the pastry and top with the asparagus.
Surround with the golden brown sauce and top with the
pastry lid and serve.

mussels
in a thai red curry coconut sauce
with coriander

For the sauce - Heat the oil in a deep pan.

Add the curry paste and a little coconut milk.

Cook until the mixture separates. Stirring continuously,

add the fish sauce and sugar, then the coconut milk

and bring to a boil.

4 portions fresh mussels, about 2 lbs.

Thai Red Curry Coconut Sauce
2 tbsp red curry paste
2 tins coconut milk (unsweetened)
4 tbsp fish sauce
2 tbls sugar
2 tbsp vegetable oil
1 cup chopped basil
$^1/_2$ cup chopped pineapple

Garnish
1 cup coriander leaves
1 red & 1 yellow pepper
(cut into julienne strips)

Wash and scrub the mussels, before placing
them into a saucepan. Cover with the sauce
and bring to boil. Add the pineapple and
simmer until the mussels open, about 4
minutes. Using a slotted spoon,
spoon the mussels into 4 deep bowls.
Reduce the sauce and add the basil
and pineapple. Pour the sauce over the
mussels and sprinkle with the peppers
and coriander. Serve with lots of
crusty bread and a spoon.

main courses

chargrilled barracuda
with sweet pepper coulis
* balsamic reduction

4 x 6 oz fillets of barracuda

olive oil

3 sweet red bell peppers

(roughly chopped and juliennes for garnish)

2 shallots or onions (diced)

2 cloves garlic

1 cup dry sherry

1 cup chicken stock

$^1/_2$ cup cream

salt & freshly ground black pepper

1 cup balsamic vinegar

4 portions of creamed potatoes

(p108 *14)

balsamic reduction (p106 *7)

flat leaf parsley

For the Sauce

Saute the bell peppers, garlic and shallots in a hot pan with
a little butter for about five minutes stirring occasionally.
Add the sherry, allow to boil then add the stock. Continue to
boil for about five minutes and add the cream and salt and pepper.
Reduce for a further five minutes and allow to cool. When cool,
blend the sauce and pass through a sieve.

For the Balsamic Glaze, index p106 *7

Brush the fish with a little olive oil and place on a pre-heated grill.
The cooking time will differ depending on the thickness of the fish.
A thin fillet of fish should only take about two minutes each side.
Place the creamed potatoes in the centre of the plate, surround
with the pepper coulis, squeeze a little balsamic reduction around
the coulis. Place two grilled fish on the potatoes and garnish with
juliennes of roasted sweet red bell pepper and a little flat leaf
parsley. Place two aubergine chips around the fish. Serve at once.

Chef's Note . . .

You do not have to chargrill the fish if you don't have a grill. You could pan fry it or put it under a griddle.
If so, lightly flour the fish before cooking. If grilling, brush the fish with olive oil and salt and pepper.

seared tuna nori roll with wasabi mash,
* japanese ginger * soy dipping sauce

4 tuna rolls - 3"x1"

4 sheets nori seaweed

a little water

2 tbsp toasted sesame seeds

salt & freshly ground pepper

1 bamboo sushi roller

$^1/_2$ cup asian vinaigrette (p107 *9)

$^1/_2$ cup soy dipping sauce (p108 *15)

4 portions mashed potato

4 tbsp wasabi powder
mixed with a little water

4 tbsp of sushi ginger

Season the tuna rolls with salt and pepper.
Sprinkle with the toasted sesame seeds. Place the bamboo
roller on a flat surface. Put the seaweed sheet, shiny side down,
onto the roller and brush with cold water. Place the tuna roll on
the seaweed and using both hands roll the tuna until completely
covered with seaweed. Using a sharp knife, trim the ends of the
tuna roll and put aside.

Mix the potatoes with the wasabi and place in the centre
of 4 bowls. Spoon around the asian vinaigrette and soy dipping
sauce and heat in the oven or the microwave.
Meanwhile heat a little olive oil in a non-stick frying pan and cook
the tuna rolls for about 3 minutes, turning continuously.
The seaweed should be crisp and the tuna rare.

Bring the bowls from the oven and cut the tuna roll in two.
Place the roll to stand erect in the mash.
Sprinkle with a little tomato concasse, snipped chives
and garnish with the pickled ginger.

thai green curry shrimp
with coriander rice
* fried basil

4 portions shrimp

2 tins coconut milk (unsweetened)

a little vegetable oil

2-3 tbsp thai green curry paste

4 tbsp thai fish sauce

2 tbsp of sugar

1 cup fresh basil leaves, shredded

Garnish

4 portions of coriander rice

1 cup whole basil leaves

1 red pepper cut into strips

1 yellow pepper cut into strips

1 green pepper cut into strips

1 eggplant, sliced and grilled

Heat the oil in a sauce pan and add a little coconut milk
and the curry paste. Cook over high heat until it separates.
Add sugar, fish sauce and the rest of the coconut
milk and bring to the boil. Allow to simmer for 15 to 20 mimutes.
Poach the shrimp in salted water until just cooked,
about 3 minutes, and add to the sauce.
Add all the chopped basil.
Serve with the rice and top with peppers.
Put basil leaves in hot oil until crisp,
about 40 seconds. Sprinkle on top of the curry
and serve with the grilled eggplant.

chargrilled tuna
on garlic mash
* coriander cream * coriander vinaigrette

4 x 8oz tuna steaks
a little olive oil
4 portions coriander cream
(p106 *1)
4 portions coriander vinaigrette
(p106 *2)

4 portions garlic mash

Caper Vinaigrette
3 tbsp diced shallots
3 tbsp tomato concasse
3 tbsp snipped chives
zest & juice of one lemon
3 tbsp capers
1 cup virgin olive oil
1 tbsp chopped garlic
salt & freshly ground black pepper
Mix all ingredients and refrigerate.
Best to be done a day before.

When making the garlic mash just add a little garlic butter
to regular mash potatoes.

To cook the tuna preheat the chargrill.
Salt and pepper the tuna steaks and brush with olive oil.

Put the garlic mash in the centre of 4 bowls.
Spoon the caper vinaigrette around the mash and warm
in the oven or microwave. Place the tuna steaks
on the grill for about 2 minutes each side (rare) and place
on top of the potatoes. Squeeze the coriander cream
and vinaigrette around the bowls.
Garnish with grilled tomatoes and squeeze a little coriander
cream on the tuna and sprinkle with coriander leaves.

Chef's Note. . .
Tuna is at its best when cooked rare as opposed
to well done.

fillet of beef
wild mushroom fumée
* leek & gruyere spring roll

4 x 6 oz beef tenderloins

4 medium size portobello mushrooms

4 leek and gruyere spring rolls

(p109 *20)

Wild Mushroom Fumée

1 cup dry sherry

1 cup port

1 cup red wine

3 cups veal stock

1 cup mirepoix vegetables

(ie diced celery, onion, leeks and carrots)

4 bay leaves

1 bunch thyme

1 cup dried wild mushrooms

jus of morels (optional)

4 oz unsalted butter cut

into cubes and chilled

Put the wines, vegetables and veal stock
in a deep pan and bring to the boil.
Reduce heat and gently simmer for one hour.
Strain the liquid and add the wild mushrooms,
reduce for another 40 minutes and strain through a fine sieve.
Boil the sauce over a high heat, adding the butter cubes
a little at a time until you have a syrupy consistency.
Meanwhile sauté the steaks in a hot pan with some butter
until medium rare (about 4 minutes each side)
and allow to rest. In the same pan cook the portobello
mushrooms and rest on a kitchen towel.
Fry the spring roll in hot oil for about 3 minutes.
Arrange the mushrooms in the centre of four plates and
top with the steaks. Warm through in the oven and
pour a little of the reduced sauce around the steaks.
Top with the spring rolls.

Chef's Note . . .
Do not pour too much sauce on the beef as it is very rich.

red snapper
salt cod & lobster potato
* saffron sauce

4 x 6 oz portions red snapper
4 lobster salt cod cakes (see p40)
flour for coating
butter for cooking

Saffron Sauce
2 tbsp diced shallots
1 cup white wine
2 cups chicken stock
1$^{1}/_{2}$ cups heavy cream
a good pinch of saffron threads
salt & freshly ground black pepper

To Garnish
$^{1}/_{2}$ lb cooked lobster
16 basil leaves
grilled vegetables of choice

For the Sauce

Put the wine and shallots into a deep saucepan and reduce by half. Add the chicken stock and reduce further.
Add the saffron and the heavy cream, season with salt and pepper and reduce to syrupy consistency. Keep warm.

Put the 4 lobster cakes into the center of four plates. Keep warm.

Heat the butter in a saute pan. Lightly flour the fish and saute two minutes each side. Place the fish on top of the lobster cake and pour the sauce around.
Garnish with some small pieces of lobster, grilled vegetables and deep fried basil leaves and serve.

Chef's note. . .
Sea Bass or Turbot is a good substitute for Red Snapper

seared tuna steak
on wasabi mash
* asian vinaigrette * japanese ginger
* soy dipping sauce

4 x 6 oz tuna steaks
3 tbsp honey
1 cup soy sauce
a little olive oil for cooking fish
4 portions wasabi mash
1 cup soy dipping sauce (p108 *15)
1 cup asian vinaigrette (p107 *9)
3-4 oz japanese ginger
1/2 cup coriander leaves
4 courgettes

Wasabi Mash
4 portions of regular mash potatoes
4 tsp wasabi puree

For the Wasabi Mash
Mix the wasabi and the potatoes together and put aside.

Using a whisk mix the honey and soy sauce. Place the tuna steaks in the honey soy mixture for 15 minutes.

The asian vinaigrette and soy dipping sauce can be made two days in advance and refrigerated.

Place the potatoes in the centre of the plates. Spoon some asian vinaigrette around the potatoes. Using a squeezy bottle, squeeze some soy dipping sauce around the potatoes. Warm in the oven. Heat the olive oil in a non stick pan, not too hot or the honey will burn. Gently saute the tuna steaks for one minute each side for it to be nice and rare. Cut the tuna in half diagonally and place on the potatoes. Garnish the dish with some pickled ginger, blanched courgettes and coriander leaves. Serve immediately.

(Japanese ginger can be bought at good supermarkets everywhere)

w curry lobster rice
* coriander vinaigrette

Bring the water and the vegetables to a boil.

Add salt and cook the lobster for 17 minutes.

Remove from stock and allow to cool.

When cool remove the meat from the shell.

For the Sauce

Saute the yellow curry paste in a little vegetable oil with a little coconut milk. Add the fish sauce and sugar, then add the rest of the coconut milk, and boil. Heat the rice in the microwave. Warm the lobster in the oven. Place in the centre of 4 bowls with the rice. Bring the sauce to boil and reduce a little, then add shredded basil. Pour sauce over the lobster and squeeze a little coriander vinaigrette on top.

Garnish with coriander leaves and grilled zucchinis.

1 bunch thyme

1 cup white wine vinegar

2 tbsp whole
white peppercorns

2 cups roughly chopped carrots

2 cups roughly chopped onions

2 cups roughly chopped celery

1 bunch parsley stalks

salt to taste

Thai Yellow Curry Sauce

2 tbsp thai yellow curry paste

4 tbsp fish sauce

4 tbsp white sugar

4 tins unsweetened coconut milk

1 cup chopped basil

coriander vinaigrette (p106 *2)

jasmine rice (p108 *16)

otato rosti
gon sauce * crispy leeks

...pper the tenderloins. Saute in a hot pan with a little
...utter until medium rare, about 3 minutes each side.
...eat between two plates and allow to rest for
...utes.

For the sauce - Bring the sherry to a boil and add the chicken stock.
Reduce the liquid for about 10 minutes, then add the cream,
dijon mustard, tarragon and salt & pepper to taste.

1½ cups heavy cream
⅓ cup dijon mustard
2 tbsp fresh tarragon
salt & freshly ground black pepper
4 portions crispy leeks

Cut the leeks into fine strips and deep fry in hot oil until golden.
Place on paper towel and season with salt and pepper.

Potato Rosti
4 idaho potatoes (peeled)
4 tbsp of mixed chopped herbs
i.e. marjoram, parsley, thyme

Grate the idaho potatoes and add the herbs and a little salt and
pepper. Using your hands, squeeze out the moisture and form 4 thin
potato cakes. Sautee in hot butter until golden brown, drain on
kitchen towel. Keep warm. Can be made in advance.

To assemble dish - Place the steaks in a warm oven. Meanwhile reduce
the sauce in a pan over high heat until it has a syrupy consistency.
Add the tarragon. Place the steak on a warm potato rosti and cover
with the reduced sauce. Top with the crispy leeks, sprinkle with tomato
concasse and surround with zuchini squares.

Chef's note . . .
Always allow cooked meats to rest so you will not lose juices when cut.

roast loin of lamb
baked potato cake
* rosemary sauce * mint pesto

4 loins of lamb on the bone

Rosemary Sauce

2 cups dry sherry

3 cups chicken stock

**4 tbsp dried or, a small bunch of
fresh rosemary leaves**

3 slices white bread, crust removed

a little gravy browning for colour

Garnishes

baked potato cake (see p.82)

mint pesto (p108 *16)

For the Sauce

Bring the sherry to a boil, add the rosemary and chicken stock.
Boil for about 15 minutes. Sieve the liquid and add the bread.
Blend the sauce and darken with the browning.
Reduce the sauce over medium heat until it thickens
and season to taste.

Season the lamb and sear in a hot pan
with a little butter. Roast in the oven for 15-20 minutes.
Remove and rest for 15 minutes.

To Serve

Put a warm potato cake in the centre of the plate, pour the
sauce around the potato. Remove the lamb from the bone
and slice into 5 even pieces. The meat should be medium rare.
Place the lamb attractively around the potatoes and using
a squeezy bottle, squeeze the pesto onto the lamb.
Garnish with vegetables of your choice.

fillet of kingfish
on creamed potatoes
* tapenade sauce * tomato fondue

4 x 6 oz fillets king fish or
any fresh white fish
tomato fondue (see p44)
4-6 tbsp tapenade sauce (p110 *21)
2 cups white wine
$\frac{1}{2}$ cup diced shallots
2 cups fish stock
1$\frac{1}{2}$ cups cream
juice of one lemon
4 portions creamed potatoes
$\frac{1}{2}$ cup melted butter

Prepare the creamed potatoes and tomato fondue in advance.
Keep warm, or heat in a microwave when needed.

Place the white wine and shallots in a saucepan and
bring to a boil. Reduce by half. Add the fish stock and reduce
by half. Add the cream and salt and pepper and reduce
slowly to a syrupy consistency. Salt and pepper the fish and
lightly flour. Using a non stick sautee pan heat the butter
and cook the fish fillets, covered, for 2-3 minutes each side.

Place the creamed potatoes in the centre of the plate and heat.
Place the fish on top. Add the tapenade to the sauce a little
at a time. You do not want it too strong in flavour.
Pour some of the sauce around the potatoes.
Place a spoonful of tomato fondue on top of the fish and serve.
Can be served with sauteed provencale vegetables.

shrimp in puff pastry
sweet pepper coulis
* maltaise sauce

4 rounds of puff pastry

12 shrimp

flour for dusting

oil for frying

Sweet Pepper Coulis

4 sweet peppers

2 oz Butter

2 garlic cloves

3 shallots

2 cups dry sherry

1 cup chicken stock

1 cup cream

salt & pepper

Maltaise Sauce

2 egg yolks

3 tbsp white wine vinegar

1 cup melted butter

salt & pepper

juice from 2 blood oranges

Pepper Coulis - Heat the butter in a sauce pan and add shallots, garlic and peppers. Saute for about 5 minutes stirring occasionally. Add sherry and boil, add chicken stock and simmer for 5 minutes. Add the cream and simmer a further 10 minutes.

Place mixture into a blender and puree until smooth.

Pass through a fine sieve, keep warm.

Maltaise Sauce - Put the yolks and vinegar into a stainless steel bowl set over a pan of simmering water and whisk continuously until it thickens. Slowly add the butter, whisking all the time. If it gets too thick add a tablespoon of hot water. When the butter is incorporated remove from heat and whisk in orange juice. Season to taste with salt pepper and put into a squeezy bottle.

To Assemble - Bake the 4 pastry rounds in the oven 350 for 15-20 minutes. Cut pastry in half diagonally, coat the shrimp in flour, fry the shrimp in hot oil for 3 minutes. Place on kitchen towel to blot oil. Pour a little pepper coulis in the center of 4 plates. Place the bottom half of the pastry on the sauce. Put the shrimp on the pastry and squeeze the maltaise sauce over the shrimp. Top with the pastry lid and serve.

Chef's Note . . .

When whisking the egg yolk and vinegar, it is important not to allow it to get too hot or the mixture will separate.

chop
rl onions

in a frying pan,
d veal chops and cook each side
ites (for medium rare).
ps and allow to rest between
minutes.

salt & freshly ground black pepper

2 tbsp fresh tarragon

butter for cooking veal

Pearl Onions

24 pearle onions, peeled

4 tbsp butter

pinch sugar

salt & freshly ground black pepper

In a saucepan, bring the madeira wine to a boil and
reduce by half, add the chicken stock and reduce
further. Add the cream and bring to a syrupy consistency,
then add the tarragon. Season to taste with salt and pepper.
Warm the cutlets in the oven. Place in the centre of 4 plates.
Pour over the sauce.

Sprinkle with crispy potatoes and vegetables of your choice.

Pearl Onions

Heat the butter in a frying pan. Add the pearl onions, sugar
and salt and pepper. Toss around and place in a pre-heated oven
until soft, about 15 to 20 mins.

Chef's note:

For me the difference between a good sauce and a really good sauce is reducing it just enough.

breast of chicken
grilled portobello mushroom
roasted garlic rosemary sauce * white truffle oil

4 chicken breasts
flour for coating

Roasted Garlic Rosemary Sauce
8 cloves of garlic
2 cups of dry sherry
2 cups of chicken stock
1 $\frac{1}{2}$ cups of heavy cream
3 sprigs of fresh or
1 tbsp of dried rosemary
salt & freshly ground black pepper

Garnish
4 grilled portobello mushrooms
4 tsp of white truffle oil
straw potatoes (optional)

Put the peeled garlic cloves in tin foil with a little olive oil, thyme and salt and pepper. Place in hot oven for 30 minutes until soft and remove.

Bring the sherry to a boil and add the chicken stock. Reduce by half, add the rosemary and garlic. Then add the cream and season with salt and pepper. Blend the sauce and reduce to a syrupy consistency. Grill the portobello mushrooms. Lightly dust the chicken breasts with seasoned flour. Put butter into a hot pan and add the chicken breast skin side down for 1 minute. Turn the chicken breasts over for another minute and sear. Put the breasts skin side down into a hot oven for about 6-8 minutes until just cooked. Rest the chicken between two plates for 15 minutes. Deep fry straw potatoes in hot oil until golden and crisp. Put in kitchen paper and season with salt and pepper. Arrange the mushrooms in the centre of the plates. Top with the warmed chicken breast. Pour over the sauce, place the straw potatoes on the chicken and squeeze a little truffle oil around the plate and serve.

cajun style salmon
on asian noodles
* orange vinaigrette * basil oil * mango salsa

Asian Noodles

1 pack udon noodles

a little asian vinaigrette (p107 *9)

a little soy dipping sauce (p108 *15)

4 tbsp chopped coriander

1/2 cup tomato concasse

1/2 cup snipped chives

Orange Vinaigrette

2 cups fresh orange juice

4 tbsp lime juice

2 tsp dijon mustard

2 tsp ancho chilli Powder

(or any good quality chilli powder)

2 tbsp red wine vinegar

1 cup olive oil

salt & freshly ground black pepper

Mango Salsa

2 medium size fresh mangoes (diced)

3 tbsp red onions (diced)

1 pinch dried red chilli flakes

3 tbsp chopped coriander

juice of 1/2 lemon

salt & freshly ground black pepper

Cook the noodles in salted boiling water until soft (about 7 minutes). Cool and mix with all other ingredients and chill until needed.

For the Orange Vinaigrette

Put all of the listed ingredients, except olive oil, into a blender and blend, adding the oil slowly until emulsified. Put into a squeezy bottle and keep chilled.

For the Mango Salsa

Mix all ingredients and chill.

The Noodles, Vinaigrette, Basil Oil and the Salsa can be done the day before.

Coat the salmon in cajun seasoning, do not add salt and pepper. Heat olive oil in a pan. Add the salmon and sauté over a medium heat for about 2 minutes each side. Salmon is best cooked medium rare. Heat the noodles (can be heated in microwave) and place in the centre of a plate, pour a little vinaigrette and basil oil around the noodles and place the salmon on top. Put a little salsa on top of fish and garnish with coriander leaves.

dolphin
on a baked potato cake
* smoked salmon sauce * crispy leeks

4 x 6 oz portions of dolphin fillets
flour for coating

Smoked Salmon Sauce
1 cup smoked salmon pieces
4 medium size shallots (diced)
2 cups white wine
2 cups fish stock
1 bunch thyme
2 cups heavy cream
juice from one lemon
1 tbsp parsley, chopped
salt & freshly ground black pepper

Baked Potato Cake
3 idaho potatoes
1/2 cup sour cream
1/4 cup butter
1/4 cup snipped chives
salt & freshly ground black pepper

For the Sauce

Put the wine, shallots and smoked salmon pieces in a pot and reduce for about 5 minutes. Add the fish stock and thyme. Reduce by half then add the cream and simmer for about 10 minutes. Strain the sauce through a fine sieve and season with salt and pepper to taste and put aside.

For the Potato Cake

Bake the potatoes in a tray covered with tin foil until soft (one hour). Allow to cool then peel. Pass through a potato masher while still warm and add the sour cream, butter, chives and salt and pepper. Mix the potato mixture well and form potato cakes. Can be done the day before. Sautee the potato cakes in hot butter for 2 minutes each side.

Lightly flour the fish and put in a hot saute pan with a little butter. Cook covered for about 2-3 minutes each side.

To Serve

Put the potato cakes in the center of 4 plates, top with the cooked dolphin. Reduce the sauce until syrupy and add the parsley and a little lemon juice. Pour over the fish and top with crispy fried leeks.

Chef's Note . . .
The fish known in Barbados as dolphin IS NOT the mammal, also known as a porpoise, of the 'Flipper' variety.

duck breast
with wild mushroom sauce & morels

4 duck breasts

Wild Mushroom Sauce
1 cup dried wild mushrooms
2 cups of madeira wine or dry sherry
2 cups of chicken stock
1$^{1}/_{2}$ cups of heavy cream
salt & freshly ground black pepper
12 dried morels (optional)

Bring the madeira wine or sherry to a boil, add the wild mushrooms and chicken stock, reduce by half. Add the cream and gently simmer for 15-20 minutes. Pass sauce through a sieve and season to taste. Can be done day before.

Soak the morels in warm stock for $^{1}/_{2}$ hour.

Season the duck breasts with salt and black pepper.
Heat the non stick pan until very hot. Put in the duck breasts, skin side down until golden brown. Turn the breast for 30 seconds and return to skin side down.
Put in a pre-heated oven at 350 degrees for about 5 minutes.
Remove from oven and allow to rest between 2 plates for 10-15 minutes.

To Serve
Slice the duck breast into eight pieces and arrange neatly around the plate and warm in the oven for a couple of minutes.

Reduce the sauce until a syrupy consistency and add the morels. Pour the sauce around the duck. Garnish with some cream potatoes and a carrot puree in a puff pastry case.

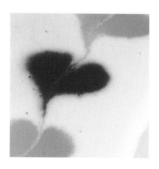

desserts

hot
chocolate pudding
with a rum cream

Chop the chocolate and melt with the butter. Set aside.

In a mixing bowl whip the eggs, yolks and sugar until it doubles in quantity.

Add the flour, then add the chocolate and butter mixture and mix until

smooth. Put the mixture into a covered container and store in a cool place

until needed. This mixture will keep for about 3-4 days.

Butter 6 x 4 oz brioche moulds and fill with the mixture.

Bake in a hot oven at 500 degrees for 10 minutes.

When ready the pudding should be soft in the centre.

For the Rum Cream

12 eggs

Follow recipe on p.98 and simply add 2 shots of good quality dark rum.

12 yolks

19 oz bitter chocolate

19 oz butter

9 oz flour

24 oz granulated sugar

white chocolate cheesecake

Biscuit Bottom
8 digestive biscuits
2-3 oz melted butter

Filling
1lb 2 oz white chocolate
(chopped)
1lb 12 oz cream cheese
6 eggs
1 cup granulated sugar
1/2 cup heavy cream

Topping
3 oz bitter chocolate (chopped)
1/2 oz unsalted butter
1 tbsp granulated sugar
1/3 cup heavy cream

one 9" spring form baking pan

Biscuit Bottom - Put biscuits into food processor and pulse for 30 seconds. Sift the crumbs into a bowl and add the melted butter to make the crumbs slightly moist. Put the crumbs into the bottom of the baking pan and using a plastic scraper, flatten until even. Put aside until later.

White Chocolate Mixture - Put the chocolate and cream into a bowl over a pot of simmering water until chocolate melts, stirring occasionally. Put aside until ready to use.

Filling - Put the cream cheese and sugar into a mixing bowl and using the paddle, mix on speed 3 until creamy. Add the eggs two at a time. Stop the mixer and scrape down the sides of the bowl. Add the chocolate and cream mixture. Mix for about 1 minute. Put the filling onto the biscuit base and bake in the middle of the oven at 250 degrees F/120 degrees C/ 1/2 gas mark for about 3 hours with a pan of boiling water on the bottom shelf. Remove from oven, cool and refrigerate for 24 hours.

Topping - Put all the ingredients into a bowl over a bain marie to melt the chocolate and butter, and dissolve the sugar. Allow to cool. Pour on to the top of the cheese cake and spread evenly. Put into refrigerator for the chocolate mixture to set. Cut and serve.

rum trifle

Soak the lady finger biscuits with the rum and place in the bottom of a glass bowl. Mix in the fruit and the jelly and refrigerate.

To make the custard

Put the gelatine leaf to soak in cold water. In a bowl put the yolks, sugar, flour and seed from vanilla pod, whisking until thick, 3-4 minutes. In a pot, put the cream and the vanilla pod to scald. Pour the mixture over the yolks gradually whisking. Return the custard to the pot and cook on medium heat stirring constantly with whisk until thick, for about 3-4 minutes. DO NOT OVERCOOK. Remove from heat and put into a bowl and add the gelatine leaf. Put into an ice bath to cool.

Remove jelly mix from the fridge and top with the luke warm custard. (You want $2/3$ jelly mix to $1/3$ custard mix). Return the trifle to the fridge. Whip a little heavy cream with a little sugar until it peaks, then top the trifle with the cream. Garnish with fresh berries and serve.

Chef's Notes: In the photograph opposite we have built our trifles in individual moulds.

8-10 sponge biscuits (lady fingers)
2 cups of prepared strawberry jelly
1 cup tinned fruit cocktail
4 fl.oz rum

Custard
550 ml heavy cream
1oz flour
1 vanilla pod
7 oz granulated sugar
9 egg yolks
1 gelatine leaf

apple tart
sour cream ice-cream
* caramel sauce

½ sheet puff pastry

3 granny smith apples

flour to dust pastry
and surface

3 oz granulated sugar

1½ tbsp cinnamon

10 oz unsalted
butter cut into 4 pieces

Caramel Sauce

10 oz brown sugar

1½ cup heavy cream

½ vanilla pod

⅓ cup water

sour cream ice-cream (p110 *22)

Thaw pastry slightly. Flour the work surface and pastry. Roll out to $\frac{1}{10}$"
thick and cut four circles (6 ½" wide). Cover a baking sheet pan with parchment
paper. Place the pastry rounds on the paper and place in the freezer until needed.

To prepare the apples
Peel and slice off the top and bottom. Remove the 4 sides leaving the core intact.
Slice the 4 sides into thin even slices. Remove pastry from the freezer and arrange
the slices onto the pastry. Mix the cinnamon and sugar and sprinkle onto the
apples with the cubes of unsalted butter.
Put into the oven at 450 F/230C/gas mark 8 for 10-12 minutes.

For The Caramel Sauce
Put sugar, water and vanilla seeds from the pod into medium pot and heat
until sugar dissolves and caramelizes. Turn off heat and stir in the cream.
Turn on heat at low and allow the caramel and the cream to blend by
stirring with a wooden spoon. Remove from heat. Allow to cool.

To assemble - Place the hot apple tart in the centre of the plate
and surround with the caramel sauce. Place a scoop of sour
cream ice-cream on top of the tart and serve at once.

MAKES 4

Chef's Note . . .
If you prefer not to make the ice-cream, it is OK to buy any good
quality ice-cream.

94

banana spring roll
with roasted banana ice-cream

For Banana Ice-cream

In a medium pot put the sugar and water on medium heat. Allow the sugar to dissolve and start to caramelize. Put bananas into an oven proof dish. Pour caramel over the bananas. Put into the oven at 300 F/ 150 C/ gas mark 2. Bake for about 40 minutes or until the bananas are soft. Take bananas from oven and check for softness. Put mixture into a blender. Blend until all banana pieces are pureed. Add to the custard (see p.92) Stir well, add liquor. Put to chill in a bowl of water and ice and churn in an ice-cream maker for about 20 minutes. Put into a container and freeze.

3 large bananas, ripe
8 egg yolks
3 cups heavy cream
1 cup of milk
8 oz sugar
2 oz water
$\frac{1}{2}$ vanilla pod
2 oz banana liquor

For Banana Spring Roll

Peel bananas and cut to 4 inches in length. To wrap, take one wrapper, place in diamond shape, and place the banana on the bottom of the wrapper. Sprinkle with cinnamon sugar, the nuts and the chocolate. Starting from the bottom of the diamond, roll to half the wrapper and brush with egg yolk. Fold in the sides and continue to wrap to the end. Make the other rolls, store in fridge uncovered until ready to fry. Heat the oil to 350 degrees and fry the banana spring rolls until brown and crispy. Cut diagonally and serve with the ice-cream.

Banana Spring Roll
3 oz roasted macadamia nuts, chopped
3 oz white chocolate chopped or chips
4 ripe bananas (large-medium)
2 oz cinnamon sugar
3 egg yolks
4 spring roll wrappers

bread & butter pudding
* vanilla cream * raspberries

Butter a baking dish and sprinkle with some of the raisins.

To make the custard, put the yolks and sugar into a stainless steel bowl.

Scrape the seeds from the vanilla pod and add to the yolk and sugar mixture.

In a medium pot bring cream and remaining pod to a boil.

Remove from the heat and using a whisk add it to the egg and sugar mixture.

Remove the crust from the bread and spread with the butter.

Dip the bread into the custard mixture and place in a buttered

½ sandwich loaf baking dish and sprinkle with some raisins. Repeat this process until

5 egg yolks all the bread and raisins are used up. Pour the remaining custard mix

4 oz raisins over the bread and leave to soak for about 15 minutes.

½ vanilla pod Bake at 325F/160C/gas mark 3 until browned and set (40-45 minutes).

1¼ pint heavy cream Serve warm with the raspberries and vanilla cream.

4 ½ oz sugar

4 oz butter at room temperature For the Vanilla Cream

Scrape out the vanilla seeds fron the pod and mix with the egg

Vanilla Cream yolks and the sugar. Boil the milk and, whisking continuously

½ lt of milk add the milk to the yolk and sugar mixture. Put the pod into the

5 egg yolks custard and return to a low heat stiring continuously for 2-3

3 oz white granulated sugar minutes. Allow to cool and remove the pod before serving.

½ a vanilla pod

SERVES 4

almond fruit cone
with pernod custard
* raspberry sauce

Pernod Custard

4 egg yolks

17 fl.oz milk

$1/_2$ a vanilla pod

1-2 tbsp pernod

4 oz granulated sugar

$2^1/_2$ oz cornstarch

2 oz water

Almond Cone

4 egg whites

7 oz Icing sugar

$2^1/_2$ oz melted butter

4 oz flour

1 oz ground almonds

2 tbsp heavy cream

Raspberry Sauce

8 oz frozen raspberries (defrosted)

12 oz sugar

In a bowl put yolks, sugar and seeds from the vanilla pod. Whisk for 3-4 minutes until thick. Scald the milk with the remaining pod. Gradually stir the hot milk into the yolk mixture. Add the water to the cornstarch and mix well, then add to the custard. Return custard to the pot over medium heat stirring constantly with the whisk until it becomes very thick. Remove from heat and stir in the pernod. Put into a container and refrigerate.

Almond Cone - Whisk egg whites in a bowl just until it peaks. Sift flour, ground almonds and icing sugar. Fold into the egg white mixture until it has all combined. Add the melted butter and cream and mix well. Put into a container and refrigerate until ready to make the cones.

To make cones - Place a silicon mat on a baking tray and put 6 tablespoons of the batter onto the mat separately, leaving 6" between each tablespoon of batter. Spread it as thinly as possible with the back of the spoon. Bake the cones at 450F/230C/gas mark 8 until brown around the edges. Using a metal spatula lift the biscuit off the mat while hot and shape into cones. Store cones in air tight container.

Raspberry sauce - In a container mix the berries and the sugar and then put into a blender and puree for 2 minutes. Strain the mixture and refrigerate until ready to use.

To serve - Place the cones in the centre of 4 plates and fill with the custard. Sprinkle with mixed fruit of your choice i.e. raspberries, strawberries, blackberries, mango. Pour the raspberry sauce around the cone, sprinkle with a little sieved icing sugar and serve.

tropical fruit soup
with sambuca sorbet
* mango lime syrup

Mango Lime Syrup

Bring the sugar and water to a boil.

Add the mangos, lime zest and lime juice and simmer for five minutes.

Remove from the heat and allow to cool.

Pass through a fine sieve. Place the gelatin in a little water to

soften, then add to the syrup and warm slightly until dissolved.

Strain the liquid once again and chill.

Mango Lime Syrup

3 cups water

1 cup sugar

To Assemble

grated zest of 3 limes

Arrange the fruit attractively in four pasta bowls and pour

juice of 3 limes

a little mango syrup over the fruit. Chill for about ten minutes and serve.

flesh of 3 ripe mangos

Garnish with a little lime zest and mint leaves.

2 gelatin leaves

For the fruit

2 mangos, peeled, seeded and sliced

2 kiwi fruit, peeled and sliced

1 punnet of raspberries

1 punnet of strawberries, sliced

1 banana, sliced (optional)

1 paw paw, sliced

stilton cheese & port

Crumble the cheese and place in a stainless steel bowl.

Add the port and mix together.

Wrap the cheese in cling-wrap to form a log and squeeze tightly.

Place the chopped nuts on a sheet of grease proof paper.

Unwrap the cheese and roll on nuts to completely cover.

Tightly rewrap the cheese in cling-wrap and refrigerate until ready to use.

Slice the cheese and serve with country bread or biscuits.

**10 oz roasted pecan nuts
(chopped)
1lb stilton cheese
3 fl.oz port**

index

sauces * vinaigrettes * oils * creams * dressings . . .

*1 Coriander Cream
1 diced red onion
1 oz diced garlic
1 jalepeno pepper
juice of one lemon
4 cups coriander leaves
2 cups sour cream

Blend all ingredients until
smooth, place in a squeezy
bottle and refrigerate.

*2 Coriander Vinaigrette
2 tablespoons red
wine vinegar
1/2 cup olive oil
2 cups coriander
1 tbsp lime juice
1 tbsp garlic, chopped
2 tbsp red onions, chopped
2 tbsp honey
salt & pepper

Blend all ingredients
together except the oil.
Add the oil slowly until
emulsified and season with
salt and pepper. Place in
a squeezy bottle and
refrigerate.

*3 Coriander Oil
2 cups olive oil
4 cups coriander leaves
1 tbsp coriander seeds

salt & pepper to taste

Blend all the ingredients in
a blender, strain into a sqeezy
bottle and chill.

*4 Horseradish Oil
1 cup olive oil
or grapeseed oil
1/2 cup grated,
fresh horseradish

Put the horseradish into
a small pot and cover with
the oil. Warm slightly over
medium heat for 40 minutes.
Remove from heat and keep
for 24 hours then strain the
oil and put into a squeezy
bottle until needed.

*5 Horseradish Cream
1/2 cup prepared horseradish
1 cup sour cream
juice of one lemon
salt & freshly ground
black pepper

Blend all ingredients in a
blender until smooth and salt
and pepper to taste.

*6 Balsamic Vinaigrette
6 tablespoons
balsamic vinegar

2 tbsp diced
red onion
2 tbsp honey
1 cup virgin olive oil
salt & freshly ground
black pepper

Blend all ingredients.
Add oil last. Place into a
squeezy bottle and chill.

*7 Balsamic Reduction
1 bottle of good quality
balsamic vinegar

Simply reduce the vinegar
to a syrupy consistency
and place in a squeezy
bottle until needed.
Serve at room temperature.

*8 Goats Cream Cheese
12 oz goats cheese
1/2 diced red onion
3 garlic cloves
2 cups sour cream
juice of one lemon
salt & freshly ground
black pepper

Blend all ingredients until
smooth and put into squeezy
bottle and chill until needed.

*9 Asian Vinaigrette

1 cup lime juice
1 cup chopped shallots
2 fl.oz soy sauce
1 1/2 oz grated ginger
2 oz chopped
jalepeno peppers
1 tbsp chopped garlic
2 oz honey
1 1/2 oz red curry paste
20 fl.oz sesame oil
1/2 quart olive oil

Mix all ingredients
together 3 days in advance
and refrigerate.

*10 Chilli Oil

6 fl.oz peanut oil
3 garlic cloves
1 tbsp red chilli flakes

Slightly warm
ingredients and allow to
infuse for 3-4 days.

*11 Sesame Soy Emulsion

6 fl.oz soy sauce
2 fl.oz honey
2 fl.oz sesame oil
1/2 red onion, diced
4 garlic cloves
1 tbsp minced ginger
8 fl.oz olive oil

Put all ingredients except
olive oil into a blender.
Blend for 1 minute.
Add olive oil slowly until
emulsified and season with
a little salt and pepper if
required. Put into a squeezy
bottle and refrigerate.

*12 Spicy Caesar Dressing

2 tbsp mayonnaise
1 tsp dijon mustard
1 jalepeno pepper
1 tsp
lea & perrins sauce
pinch tobasco
juice of one lemon
1 tsp capers
8 anchovies
10 garlic cloves, lightly
sauteed
2 cups olive oil
2 tbsp red wine vinegar

Put all ingredients, except the
oil and vinegar, into a food
processor. Process adding the
oil slowly and then the
vinegar. Strain into a squeezy
bottle and chill.

*13 Sweetcorn & Basil Sauce

2 cups sweet corn
and its water
1 cup chicken stock
1 1/2 cups cream
3 diced shallots
salt & freshly ground
black pepper
4 tbls finely
shredded basil leaves

Sweat the diced shallots in
a little butter for 2 minutes.
Add the sweet corn and its
water, the chicken stock and
bring to a boil. Simmer for
10 minutes and add the
cream. Simmer for a further
10 minutes and remove from
heat then strain the liquid.
Add half the sweet corn
back to the liquid and pulse
in a blender and strain
again. Reduce the sauce
and add the basil.

index
sauces * vinaigrettes * oils
* creams * dressings . . .

*14 Creamed Potatoes
4-6 idaho potatoes, peeled
1/2 cup cream
1/2 cup milk
1/2 cup butter
salt & freshly ground
black pepper

Cook the potatoes until soft
and strain off the water.
Pass through a potato
masher while still hot.
Add the warm cream and
milk stirring continuously and
then add the butter and
season to taste.

*15 Soy Dipping Sauce
1/4 cup onions, chopped
4 garlic cloves, minced
3 star anisse
3 thin slices ginger root
2 tsp sichaun peppercorns
2 tbsp vegetable oil
1/2 cup white wine
1/2 cup white wine vinegar
1/4 cup soy sauce
1/2 cup teriyaki sauce
1/2 cup ketchup
1/4 cup chicken stock
1/4 cup tamari sauce
1 cup castor sugar
1 tsp corn starch
1 tbsp water

Heat oil in a skillet, add the
onion, garlic, ginger, star
anise and peppercorns.
Cook over high heat stirring
until the onion is soft and
translucent. Set aside.
Place 2 tablespoons of stock
and sugar in a medium
sauce pan and cook stirring
constantly over medium high
heat until mixture is
caramelized. Add the vinegar
and the wine to the sugar
mixture and continue to cook
stirring until all the sugar is
dissolved. Stir in the onion
mixture, soy, tamari sauce,
ketchup and the remaining
stock and cook over high
heat for 5 minutes until all
the flavours are blended.
Combine the corn starch and
water in a bowl, mixing
thoroughly add to the sauce.
Season with a little salt.
Cook over low heat until
sauce is reduced by half
(30 minutes). Strain the
sauce and discard the solids.
The sauce will keep for
1 week in the refrigerator.

*16 Mint Pesto
1/2 cup fresh mint leaves
1/3 cup prepared mint sauce
3 tbsp roasted pine nuts
2 tbsp white wine vinegar
pinch sugar (optional)
1/3 cup olive oil

Put all ingredients except the
oil into a blender and puree.
Add the oil slowly until
smooth. Place into a squeezy
bottle until needed.

When making Basil Pesto,
follow this recipe omitting
mint leaves and mint sauce.
Replace with 1/2 cup fresh
basil leaves.

*17 Tomato Salsa
4 plum tomatoes diced
2 tsp red onion, diced
1/2 a jalapeno pepper, diced
1/4 cup chopped coriander
juice of 1 lemon
salt & freshly ground black
pepper

Mix all ingredients together
and refrigerate until needed.

*18 White Truffle Vinaigrette
$1/2$ cup dry sherry
or madeira wine
$1^1/2$ cups mixed diced celery,
carrots and shallots
$1/2$ cup olive oil
1 sprig thyme
1 bay leaf
$1/2$ cup chicken stock
$1/4$ cup sherry vinegar
$1/4$ cup white truffle oil
salt & pepper
$1/4$ cup chopped herbs
(tarragon, chives and parsley)

Saute the vegetables in a
little olive oil until tender.
Add bay leaf and thyme.
Add the chicken stock and
sherry, and reduce for about
3 minutes. Strain the liquid
into a stainless steel bowl
and allow to cool. When cool
whisk in the sherry vinegar,
olive oil and truffle oil.
Season to taste with salt and
pepper and chopped herbs.

***19 Chargrilled Red Pepper
Vinaigrette**
3 red bell peppers,
chargrilled and seeds
removed
$1/2$ red onion, diced
1 tbsp ancho chilli powder
(or any good quality chilli)
juice of one lemon
1 tbsp red wine vinegar
$3/4$ cup olive oil
salt & freshly ground black
pepper

Place all ingredients, except
the oil, into a food processor
and process adding the oil
slowly. Then place the
vinaigrette into a blender
and pulse until smooth.
Place into a squeezy bottle
and chill.

For Chargrilled Yellow Pepper
Vinaigrette, follow recipe as
above, using yellow peppers.

***20 Leek and Gruyere
Spring Roll (4 rolls)**
4 spring roll wrappers
2 cups leeks, sliced,
green parts only
3 shallots, diced
1 cup grated gruyere cheese
pinch sugar
salt & freshly ground black
pepper
1 egg yolk
a little butter

Heat the butter in a frying
pan and add the diced
shallots. Cook until soft then
add the leeks. Saute over a
medium heat until soft and
season with salt, pepper and
sugar. Allow to cool then mix
with the cheese.
Place the spring roll wrapper
on a flat surface in a
diamond position. Put a
little of the leek mixture
across the lower point
leaving a little space of the
point uncovered to allow it
to come up and over the
leeks. Brush the three
remaining corners with the
egg yolk. Fold the lower
corner over the leeks then
fold the two side corners
to the centre and roll into
neat rolls. Place the rolls
into hot oil (350 degrees)
until golden brown.

index
sauces * vinaigrettes * oils
* creams * dressings . . .

*21 Tapenade Sauce
    2 cups white wine
    2 cups fish stock
    2 shallots diced
    1¹/₂ cups heavy cream
    salt & freshly ground
    black pepper

    Tapenade
    1 cup black olives
    2 cloves garlic
    1 tbsp capers
    1 tbsp anchovies
    1 cup olive oil

Place all ingredients
in a blender and pulse
until smooth.

In a saucepan reduce the
white wine and shallots until
almost dry. Add the fish stock
and reduce by half. Add the
cream and reduce until it
reaches a syrupy consistency.
Stir in the tapenade a little at
a time. Finish the sauce with
a little lemon juice.

*22 Sour Cream Ice-cream
    1lt milk
    1lb granulated sugar
    ¹/₂ vanilla pod
    juice from 2 lemons
    ¹/₂ lt heavy cream
    6 egg yolks
    1lb 2 oz sour cream

In a medium bowl put the 6
yolks, 2 oz milk, sugar and the
seeds from the pod. Whisk for
3-4 minutes until thick.
Scald the milk, cream and pod.
Pour the mixture over the
yolks, gradually whisking.
Return the custard to the pot
and cook on low heat
stirring constantly with a
wooden spoon until thickened
slightly. Do not overcook or
allow the custard to boil.
Remove from heat. Put into a
bowl over an ice bath. When
cool, stir in the sour cream and
lemon juice.
Place the mixture into an
ice-cream maker, churn for
about 20 minutes and freeze.